FLOWER AND PAISLEY DESIGNS

Stress Relief

Paisley

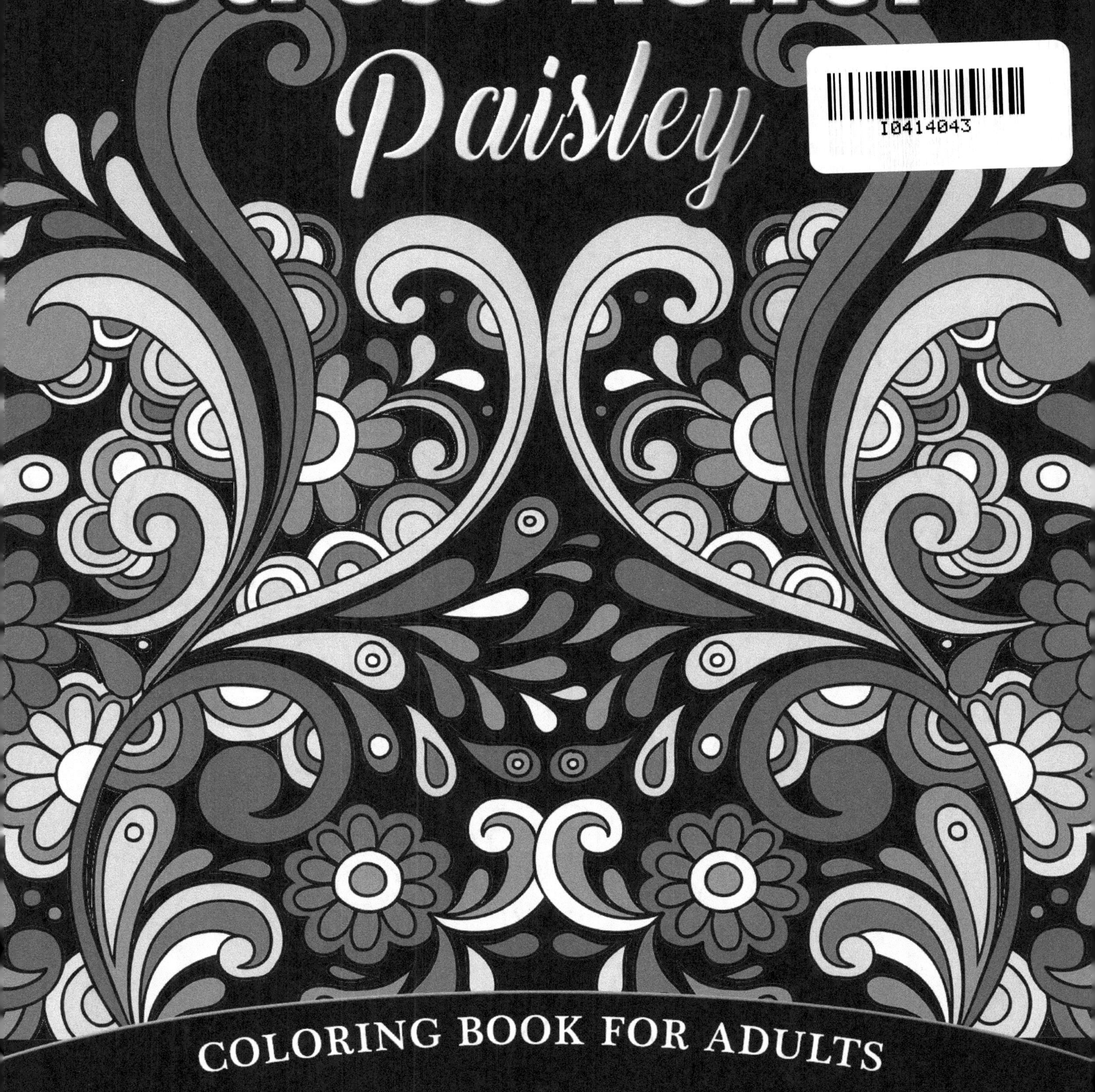

I0414043

COLORING BOOK FOR ADULTS

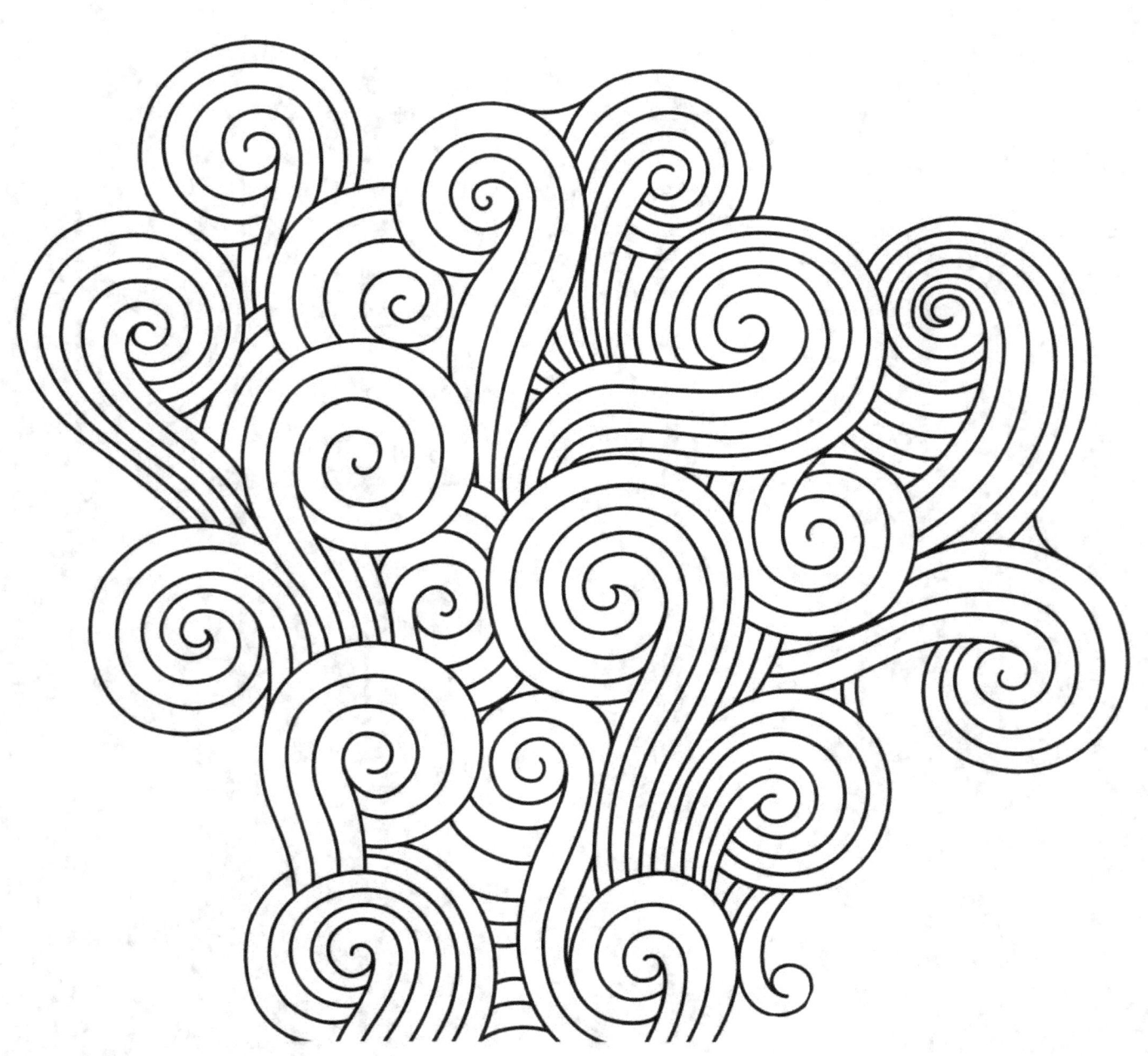

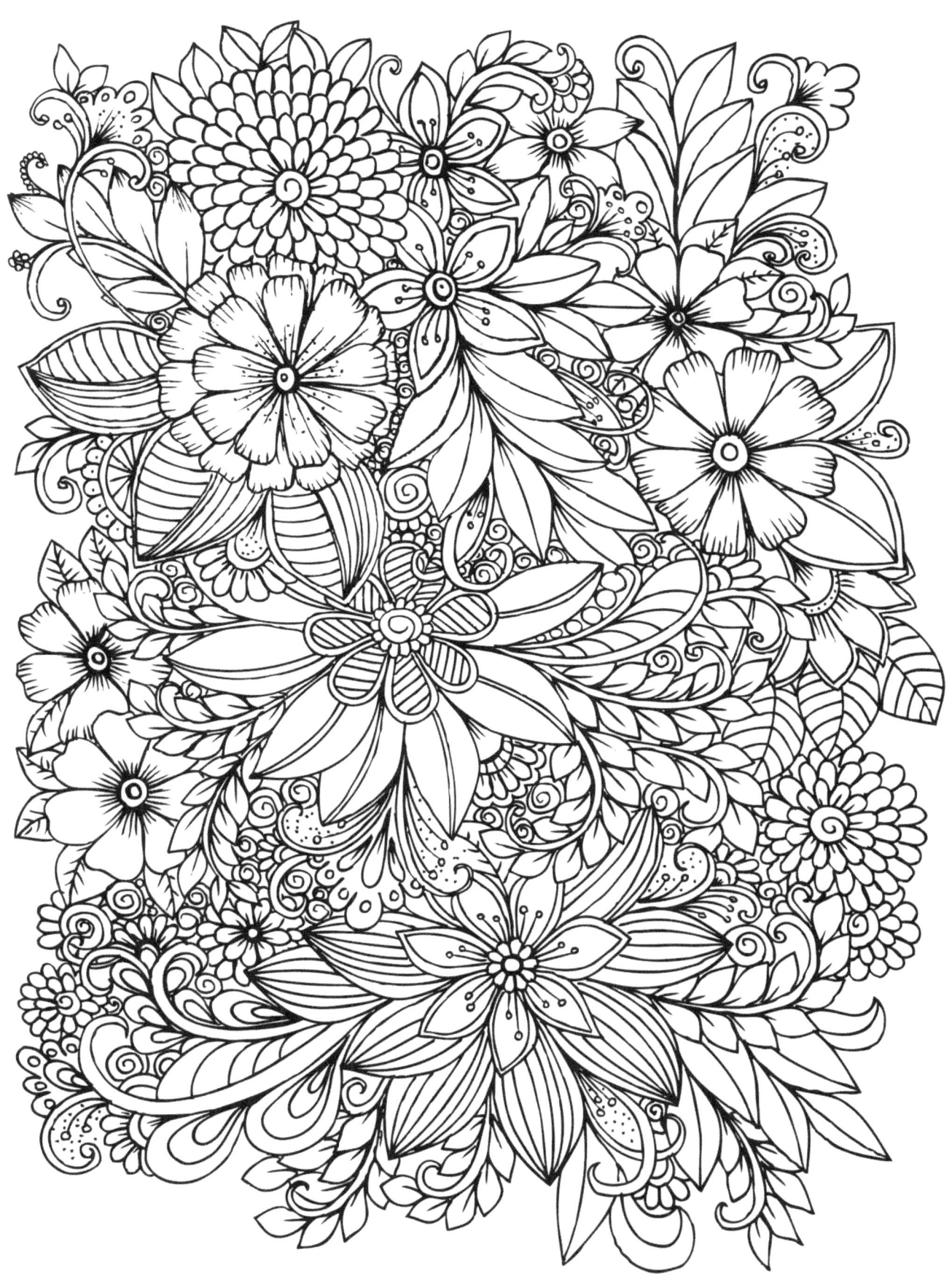

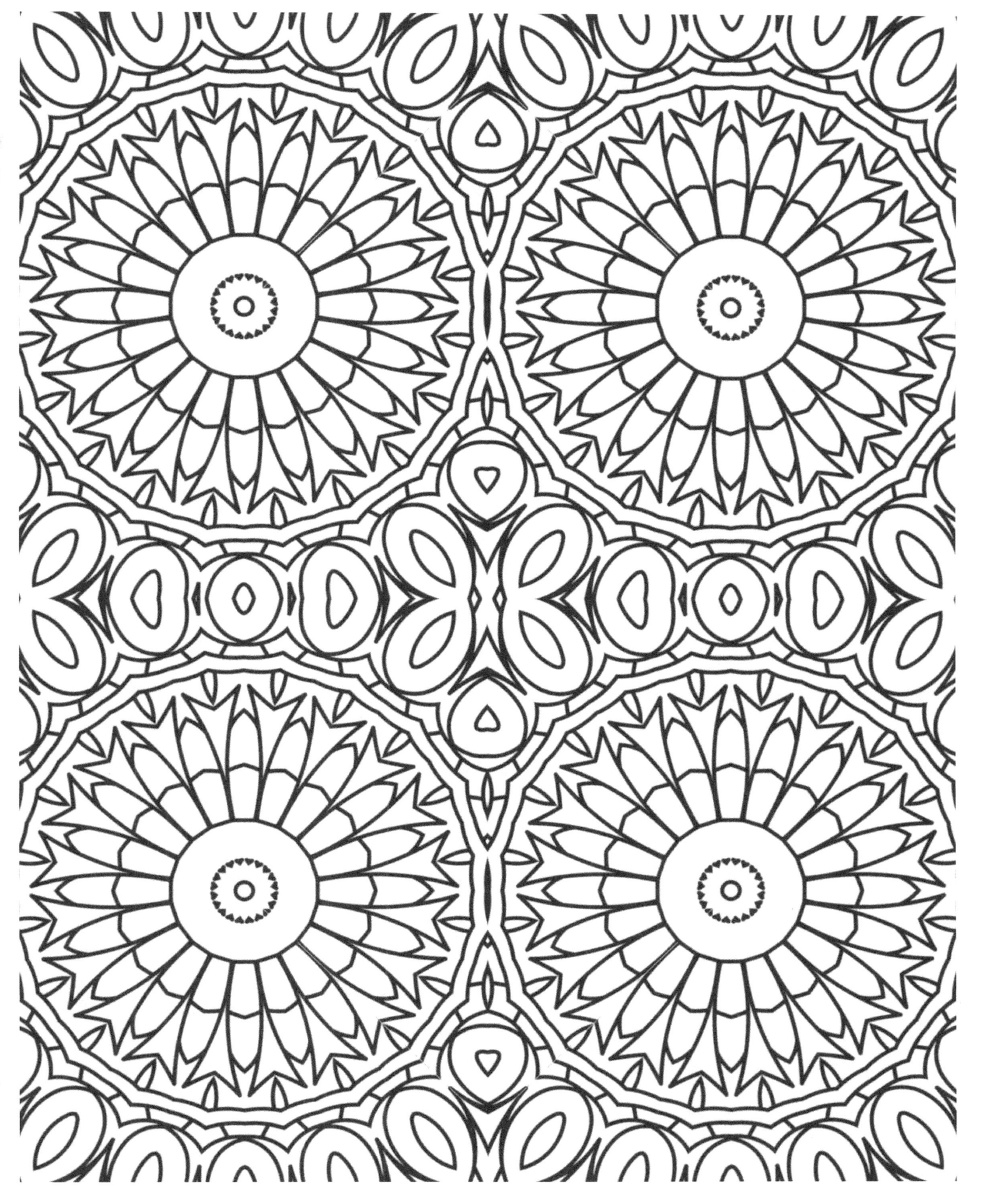

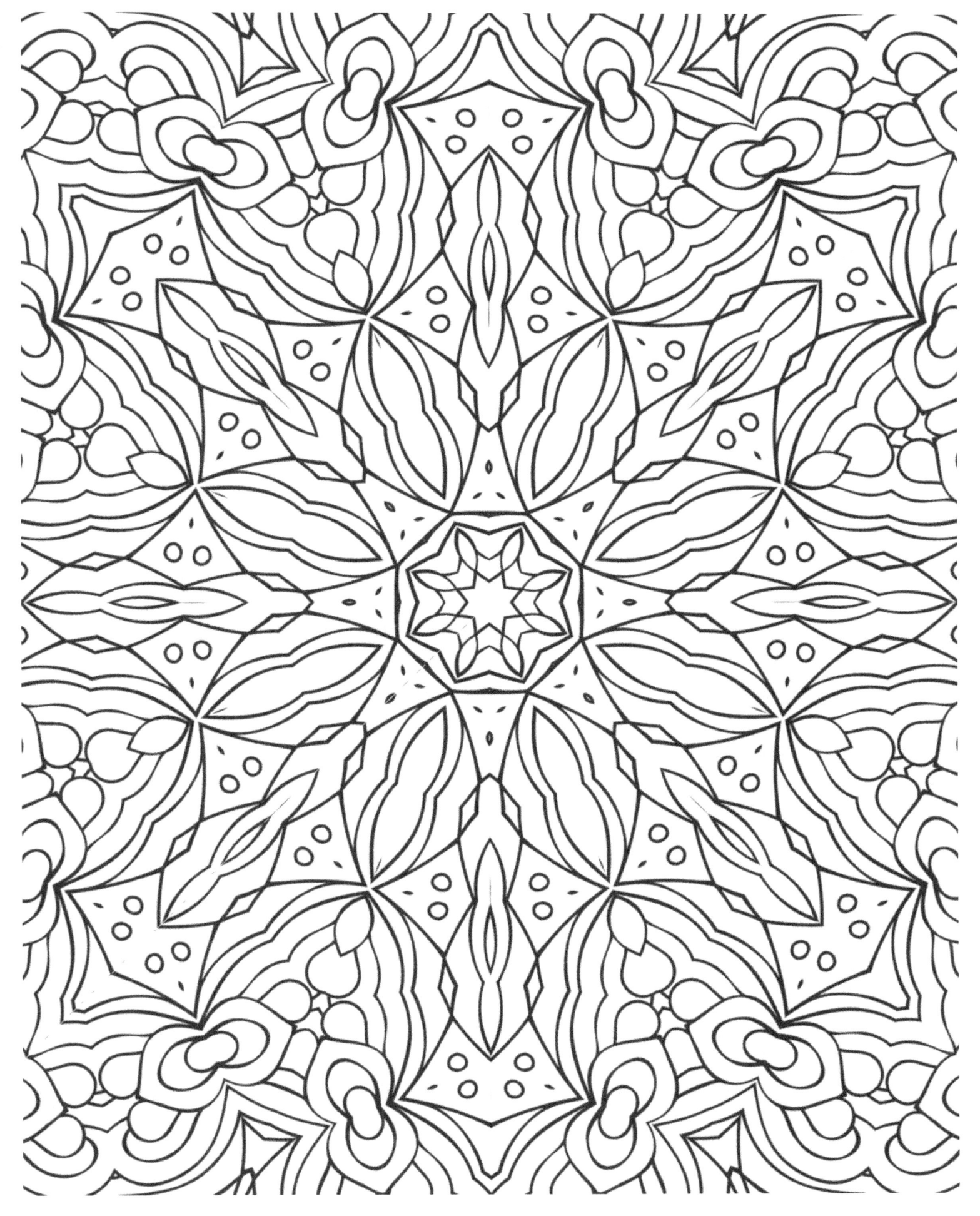

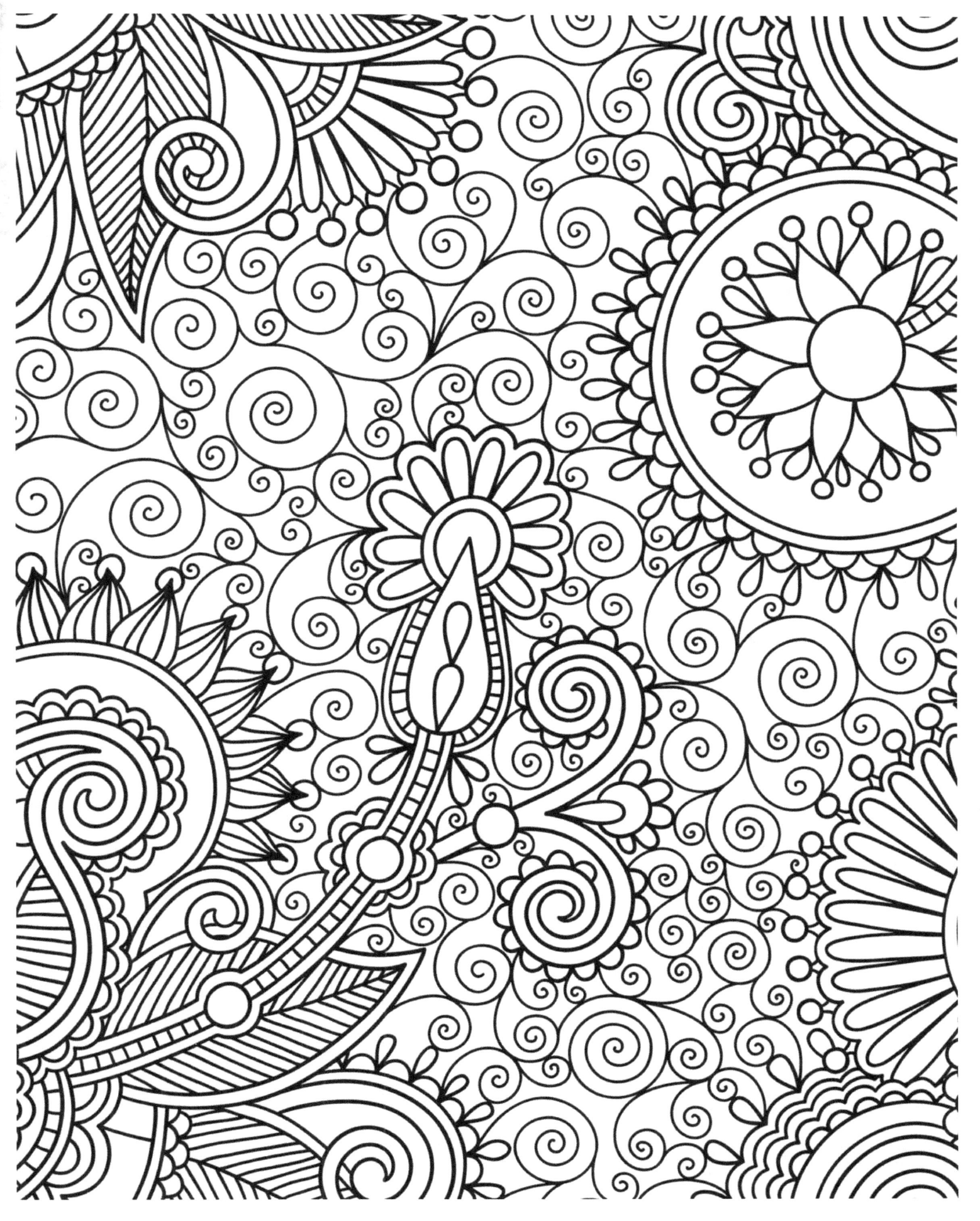

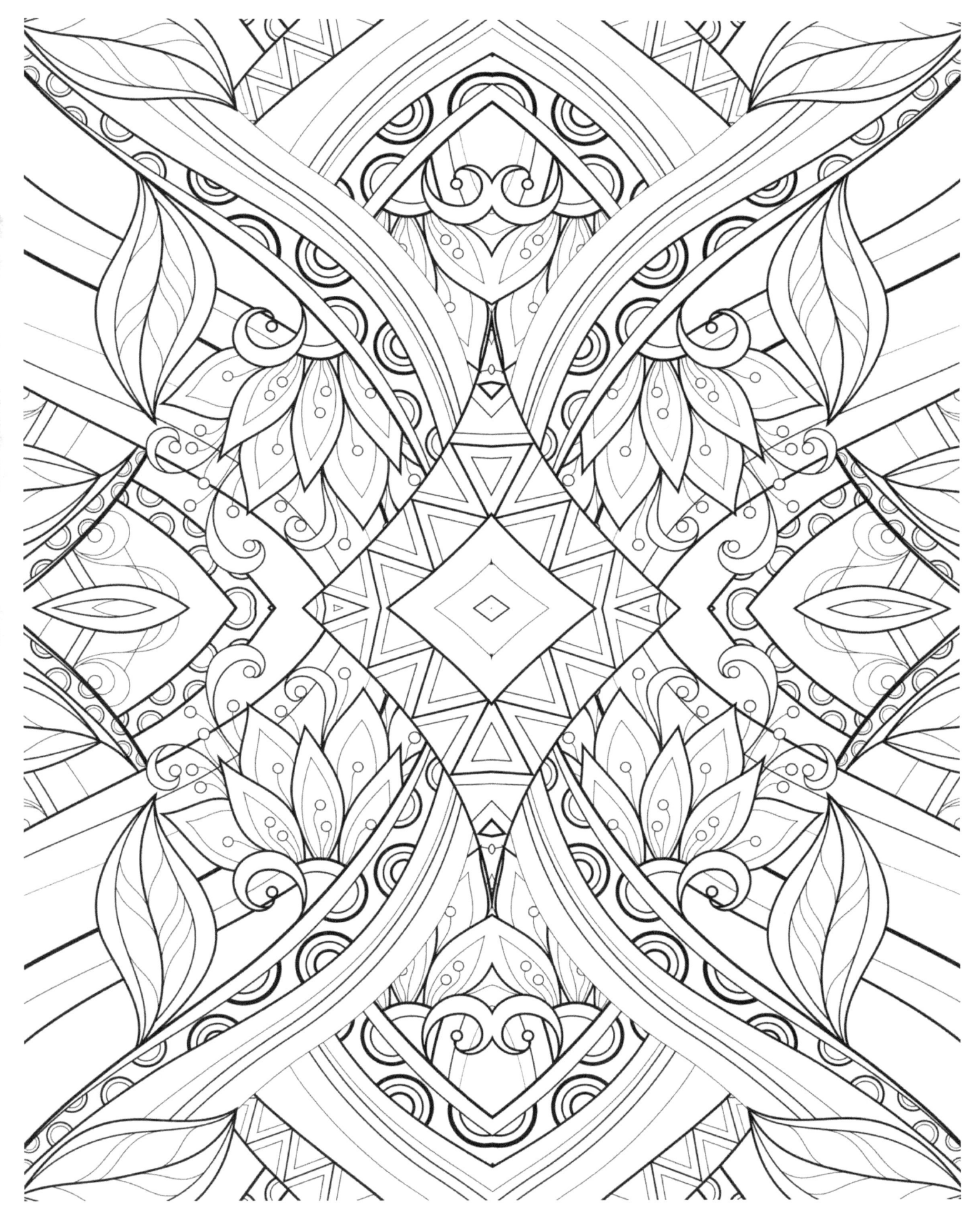

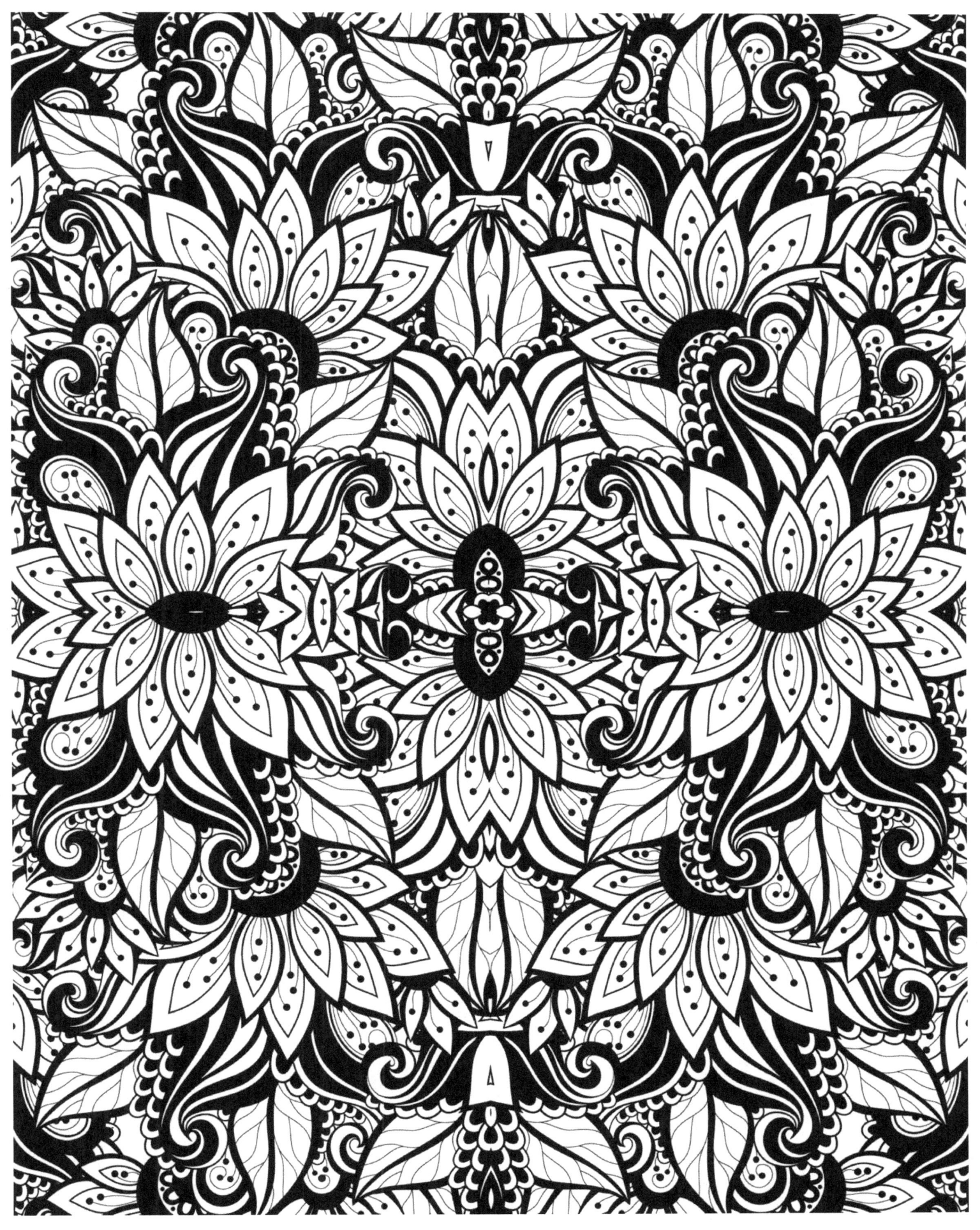

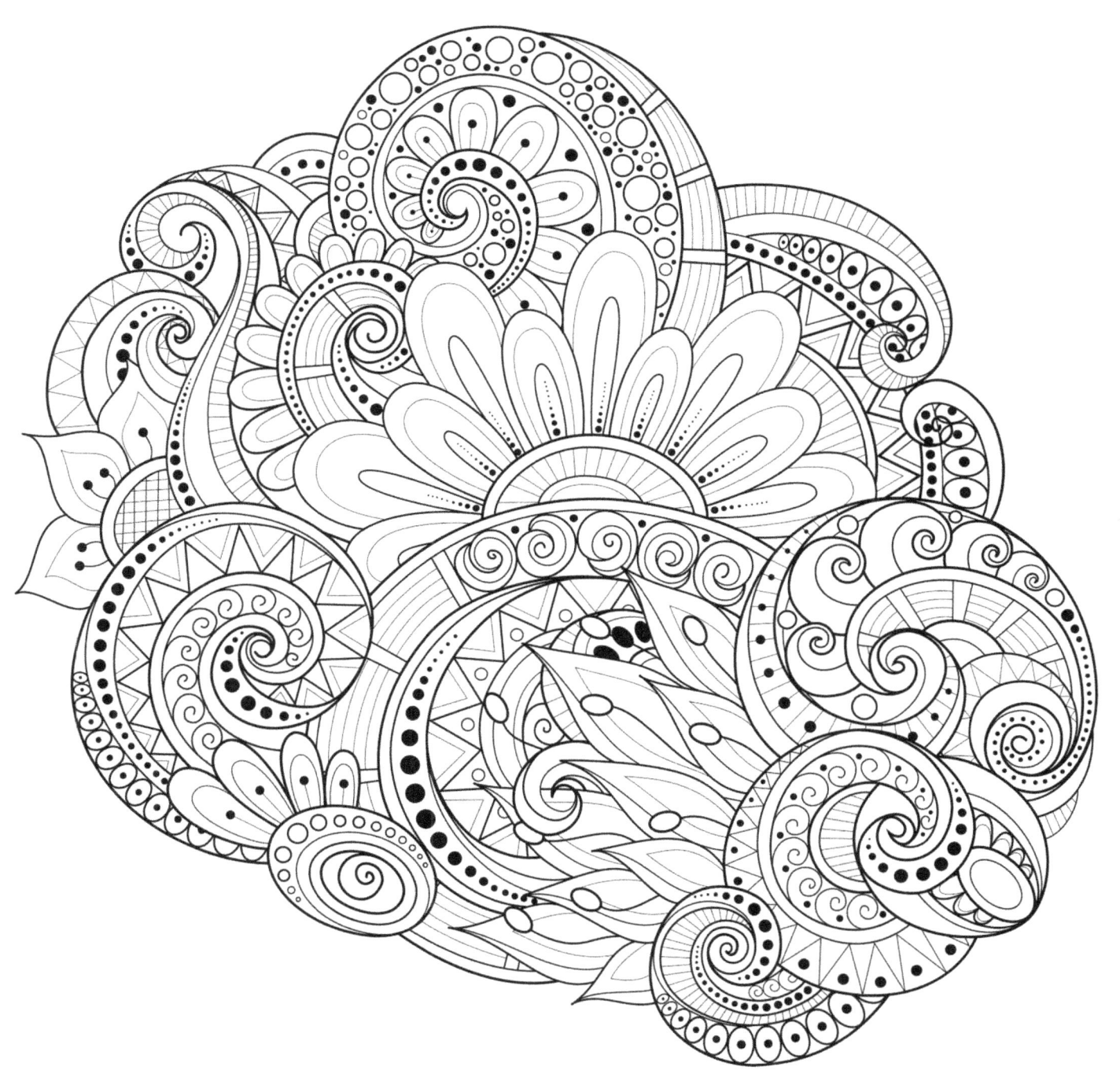

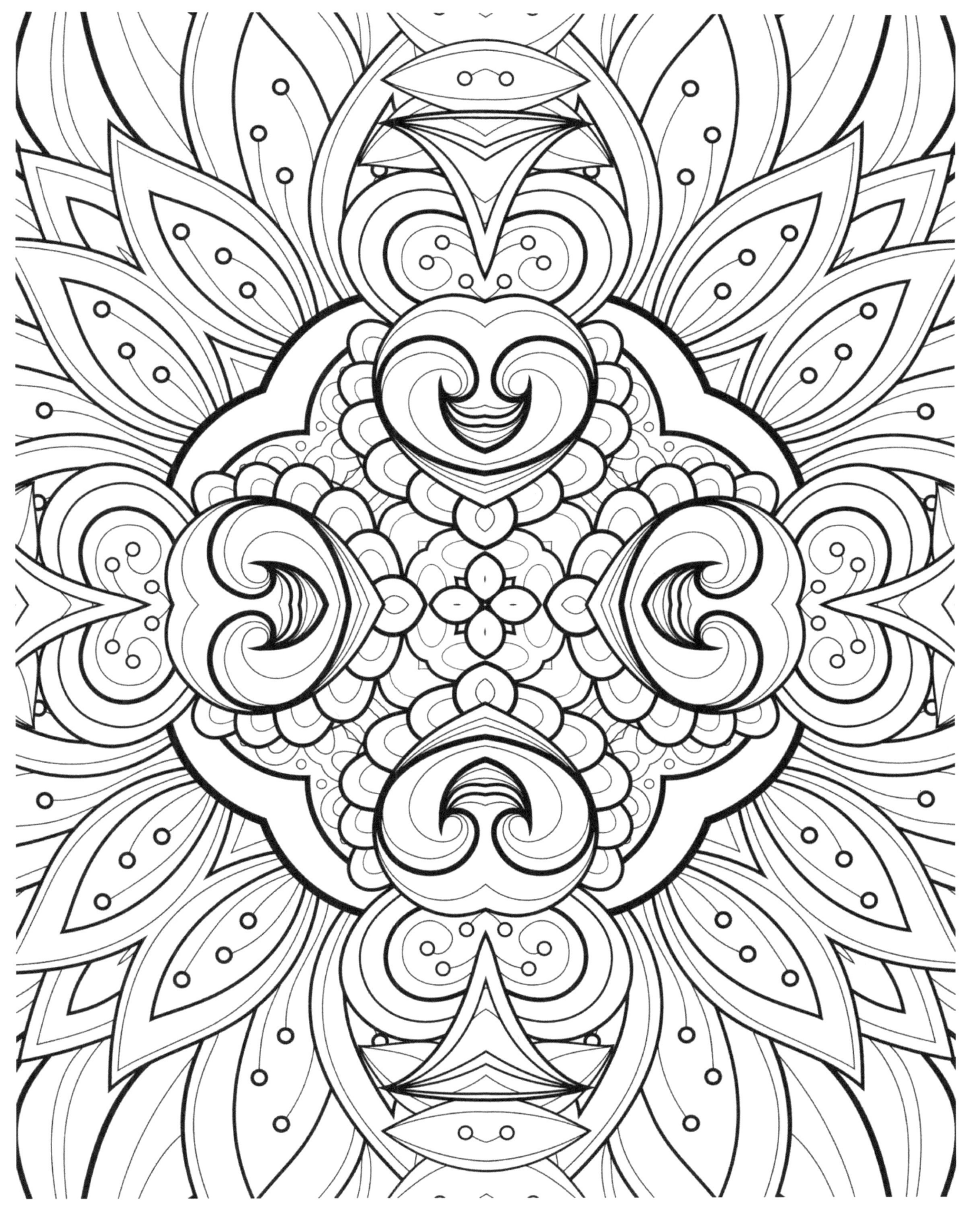

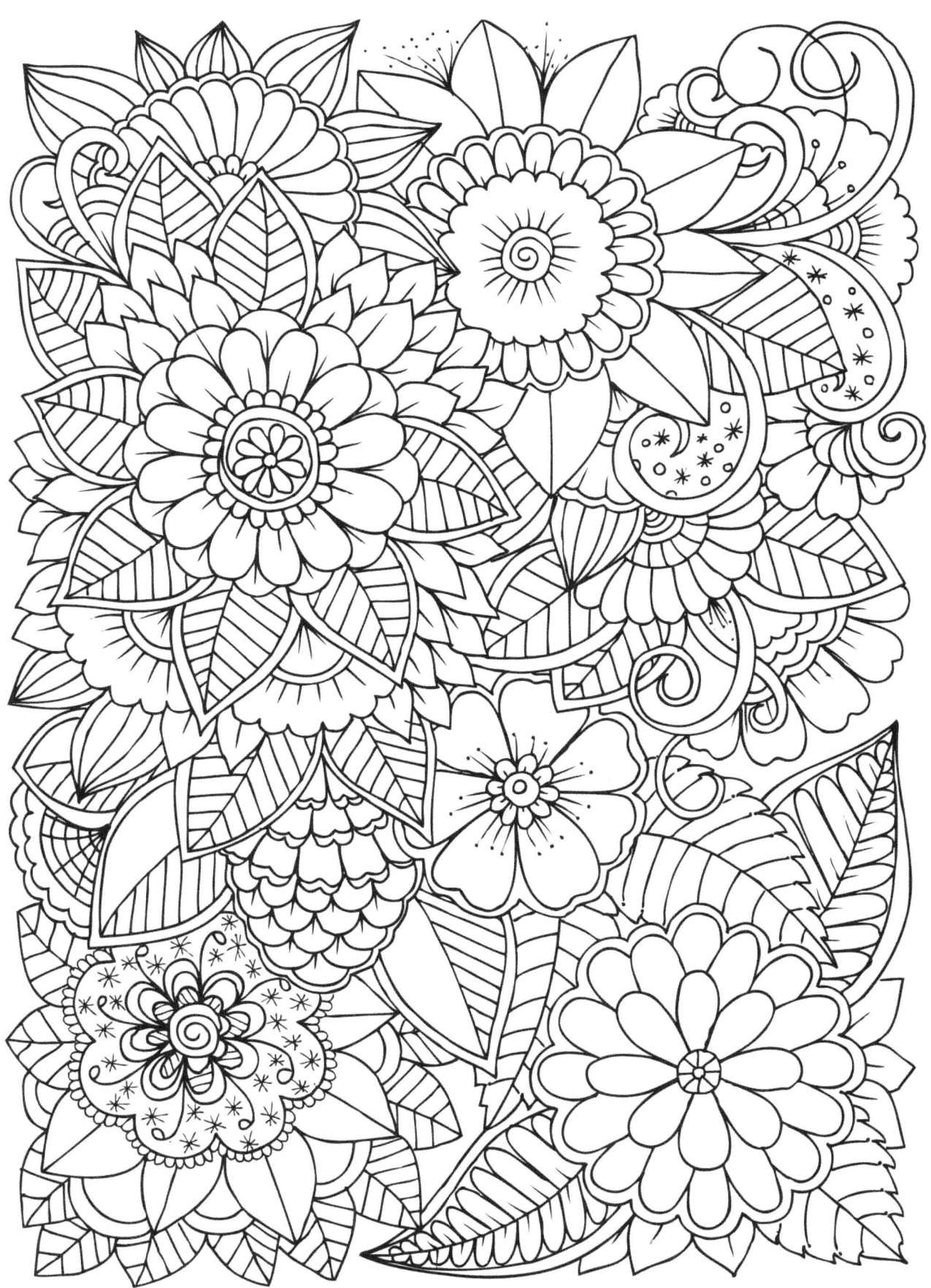

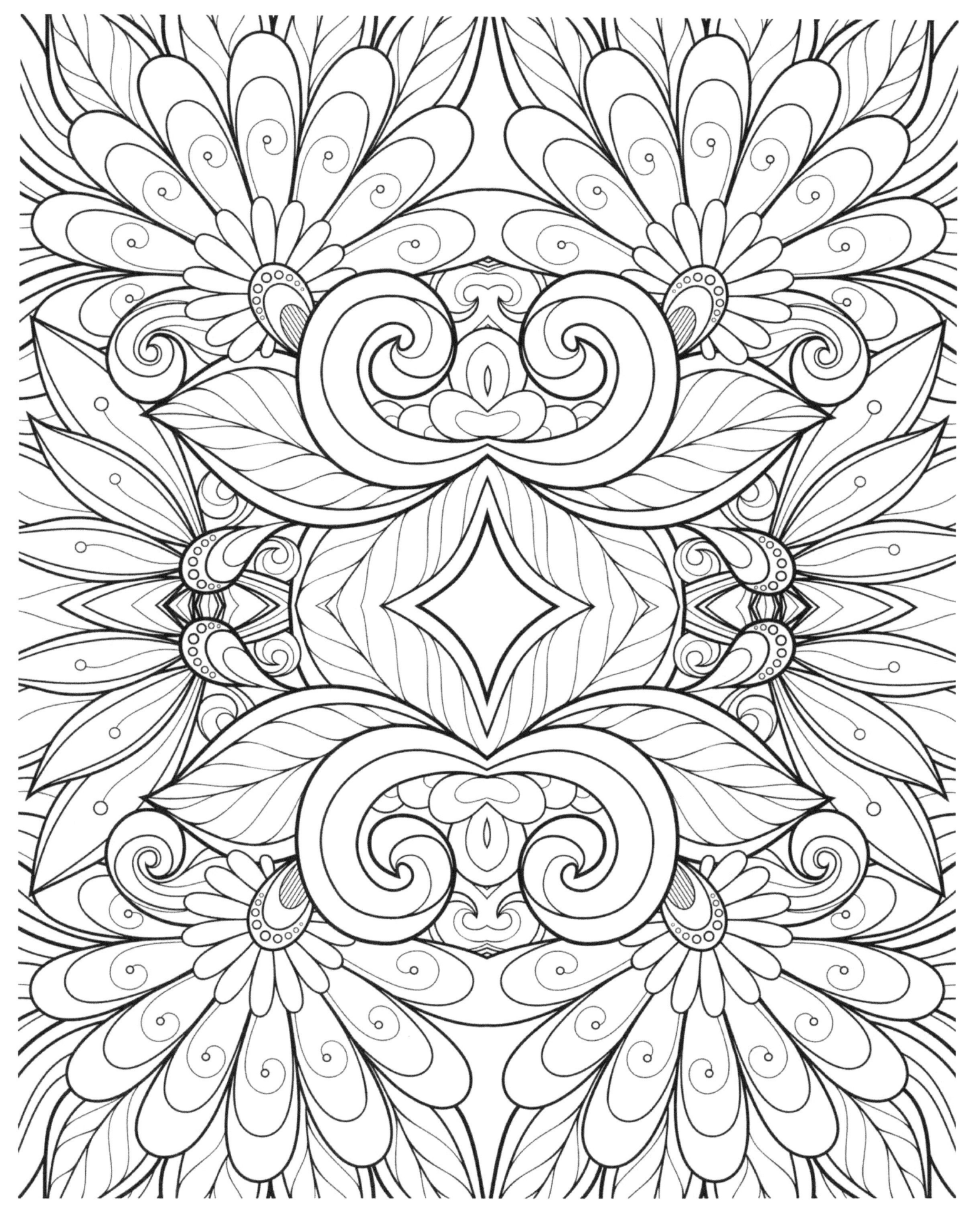

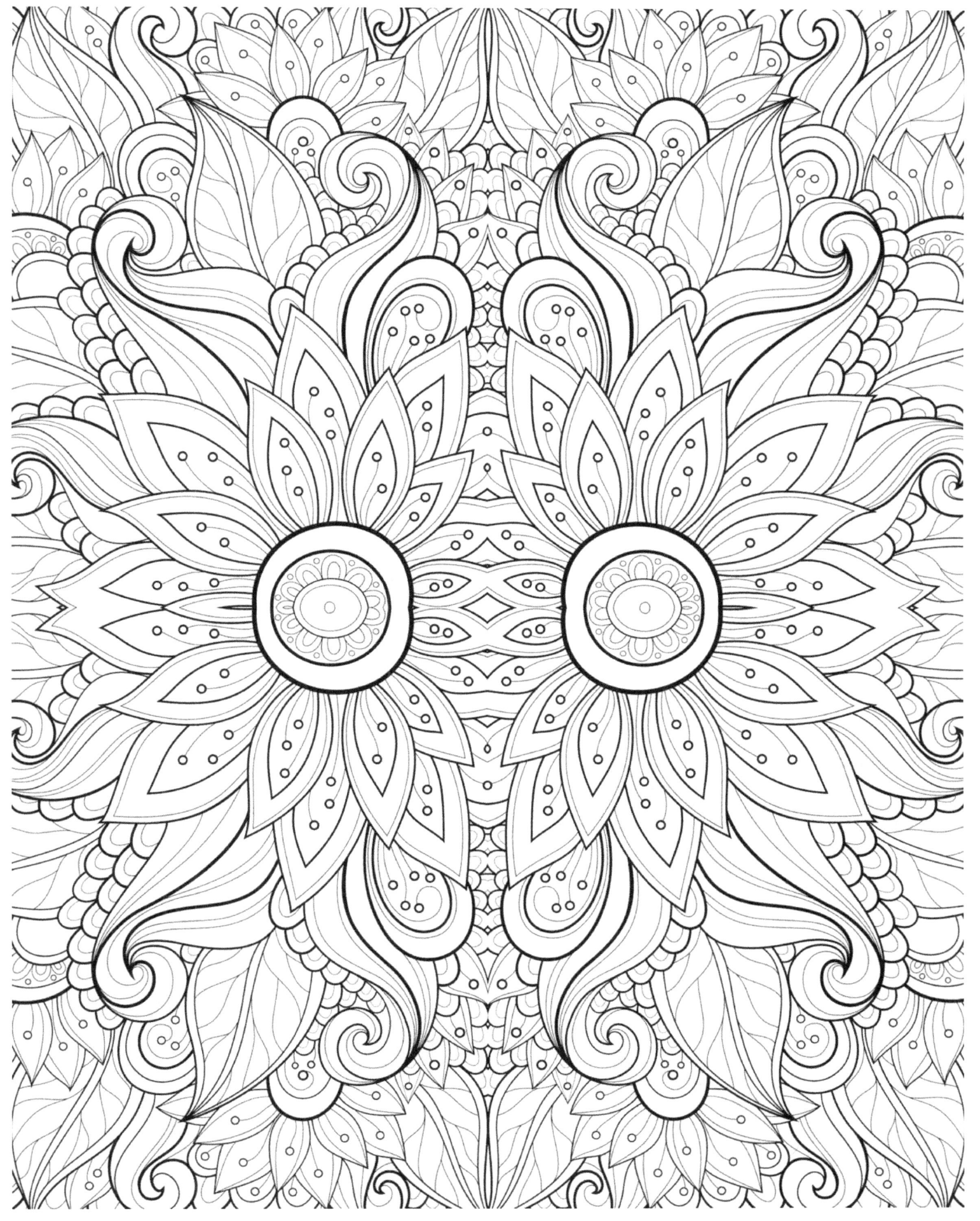

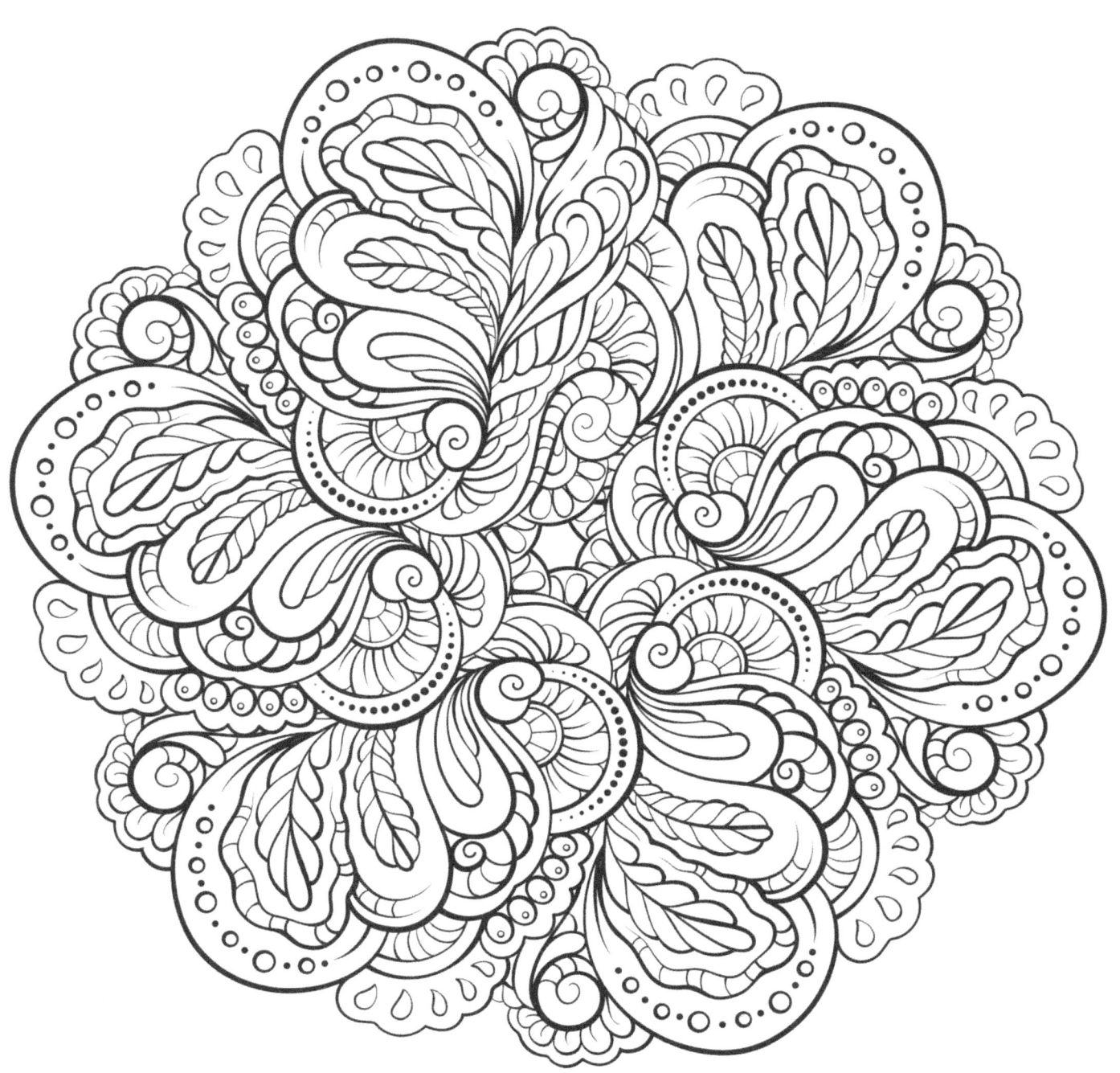

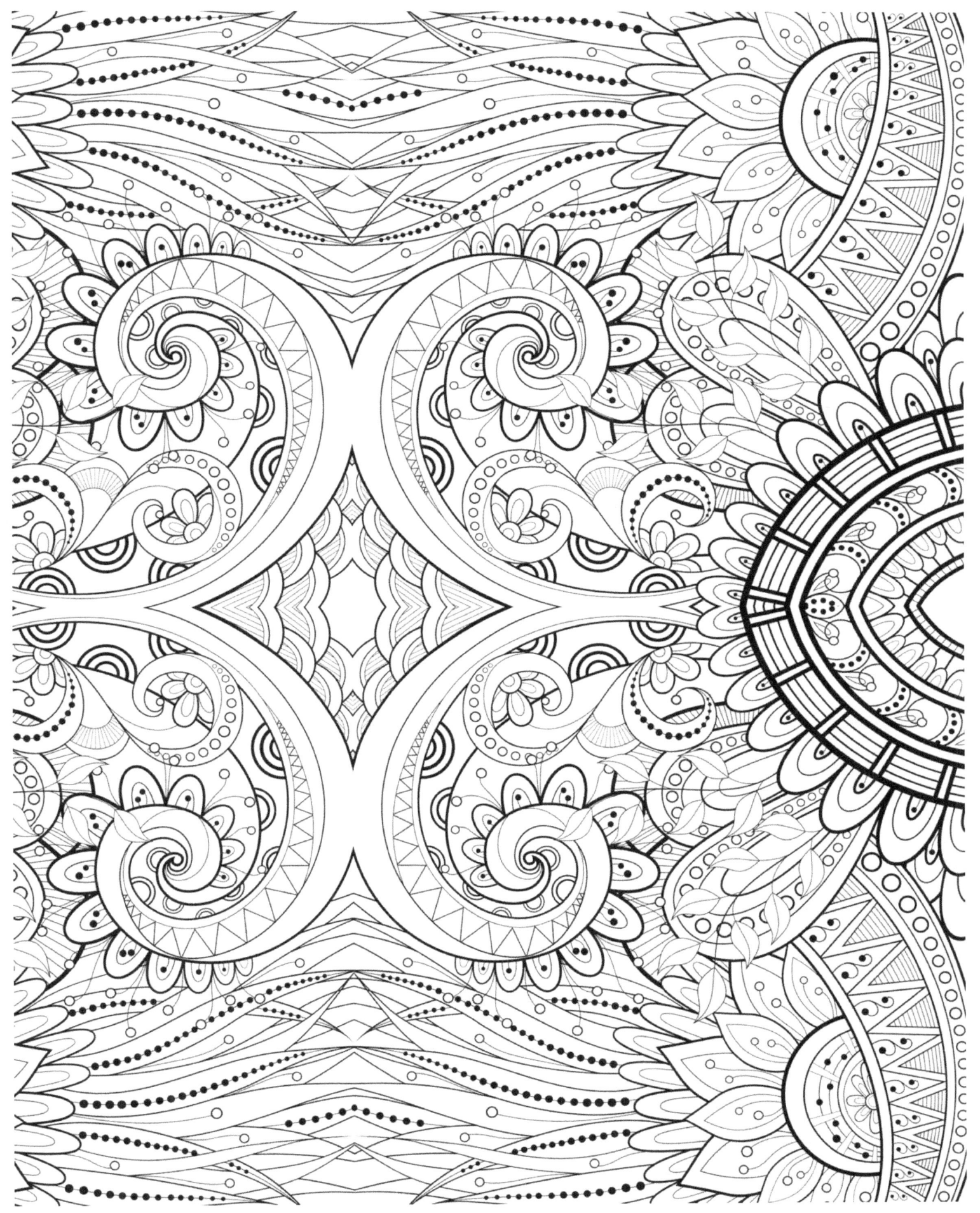

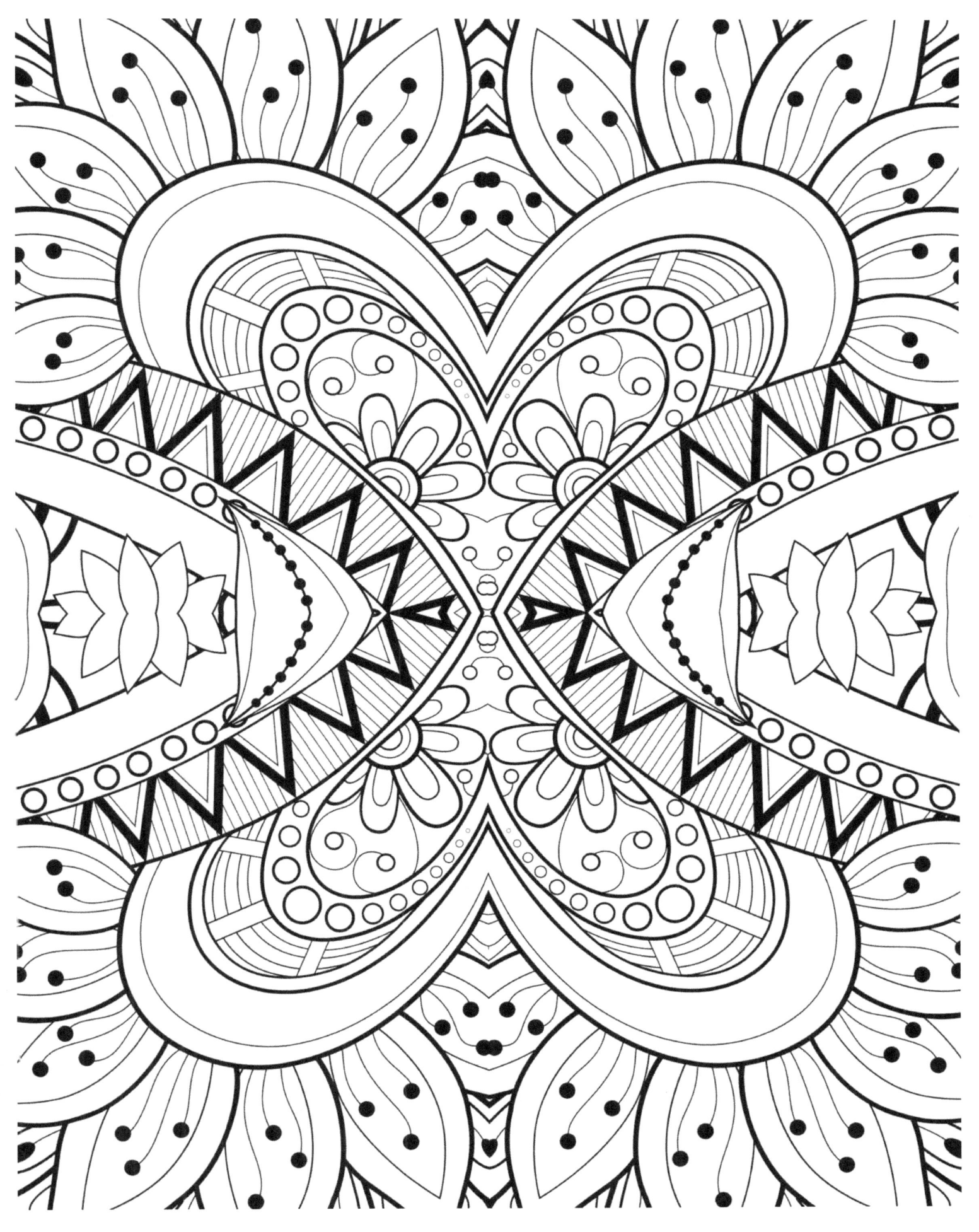

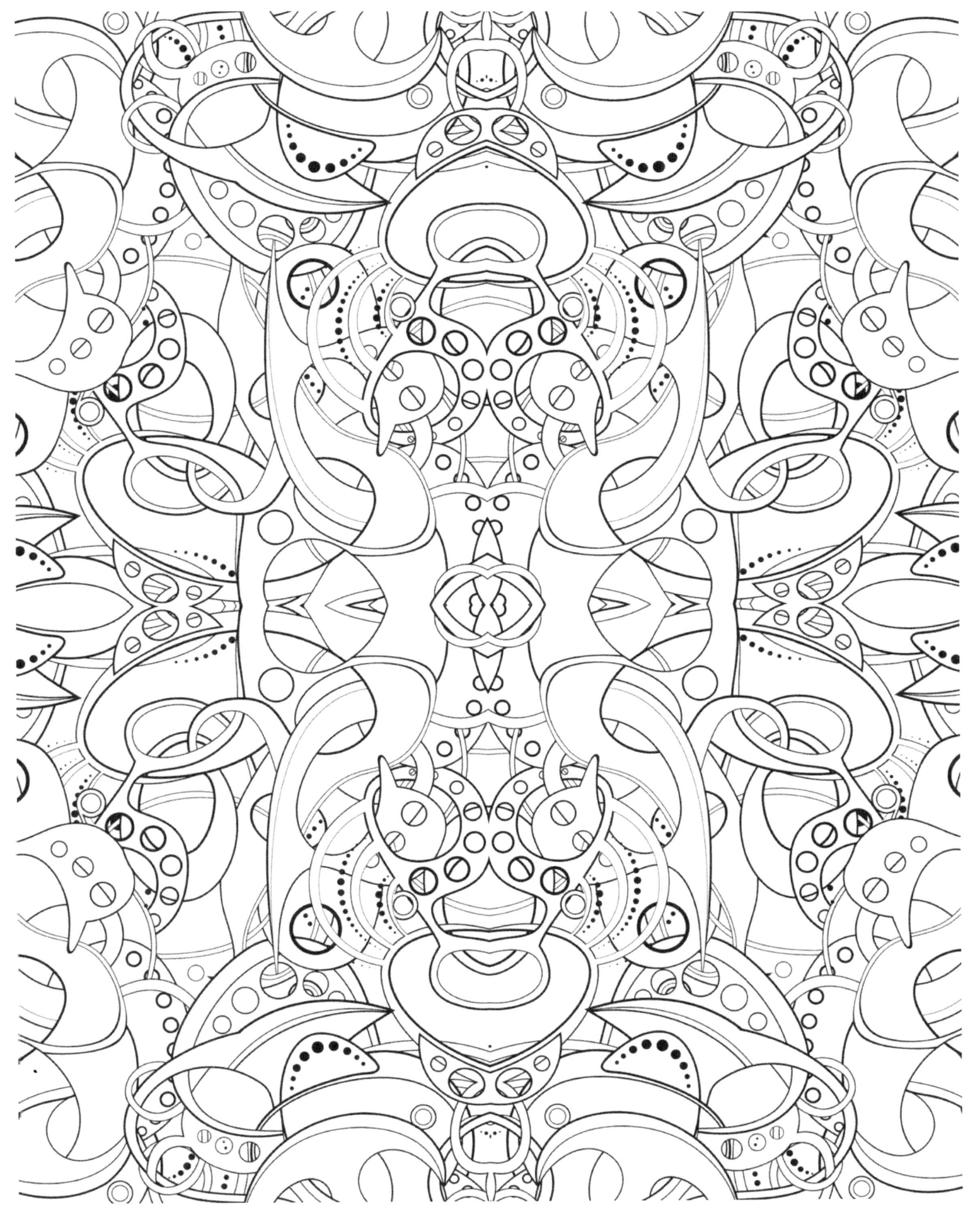

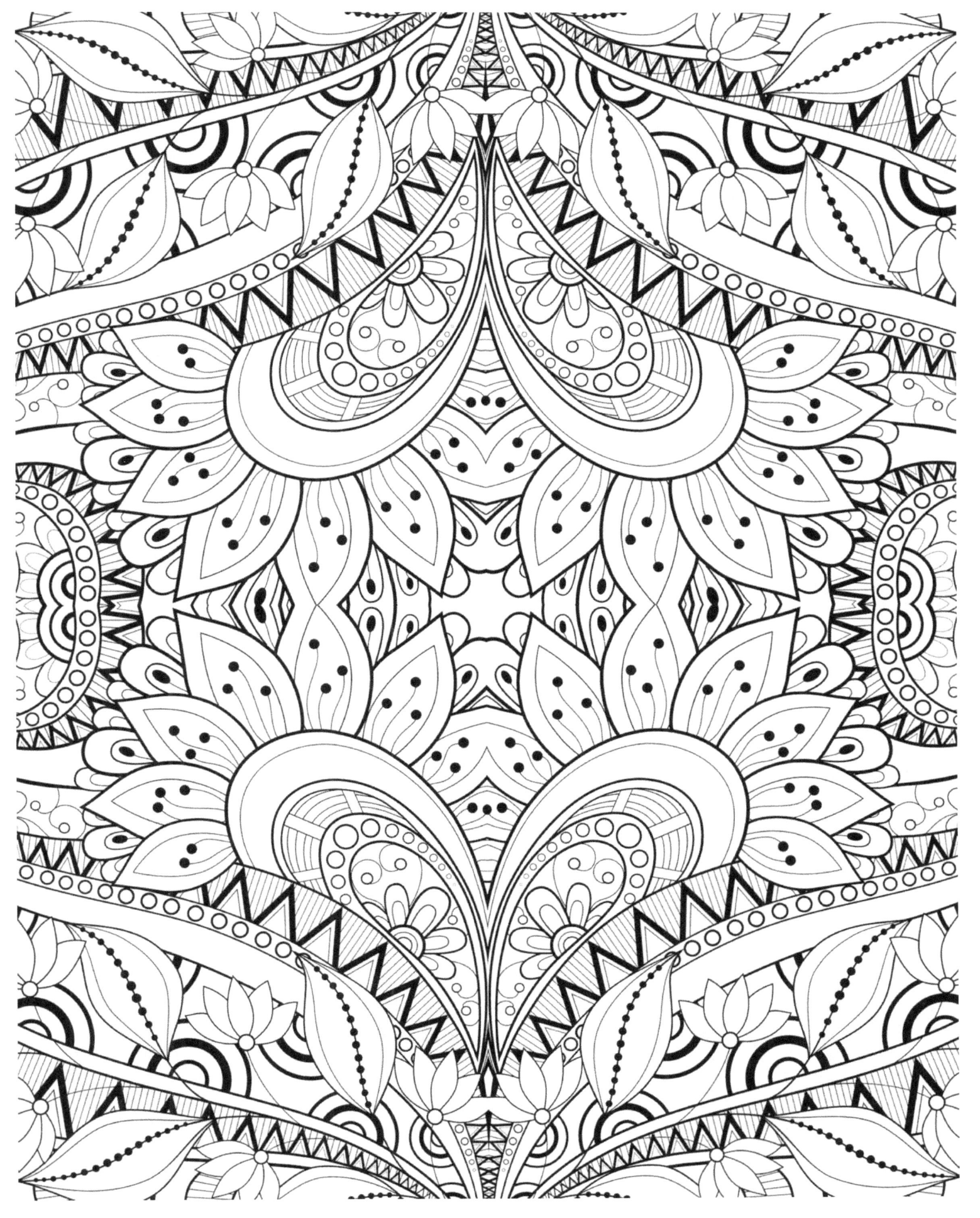

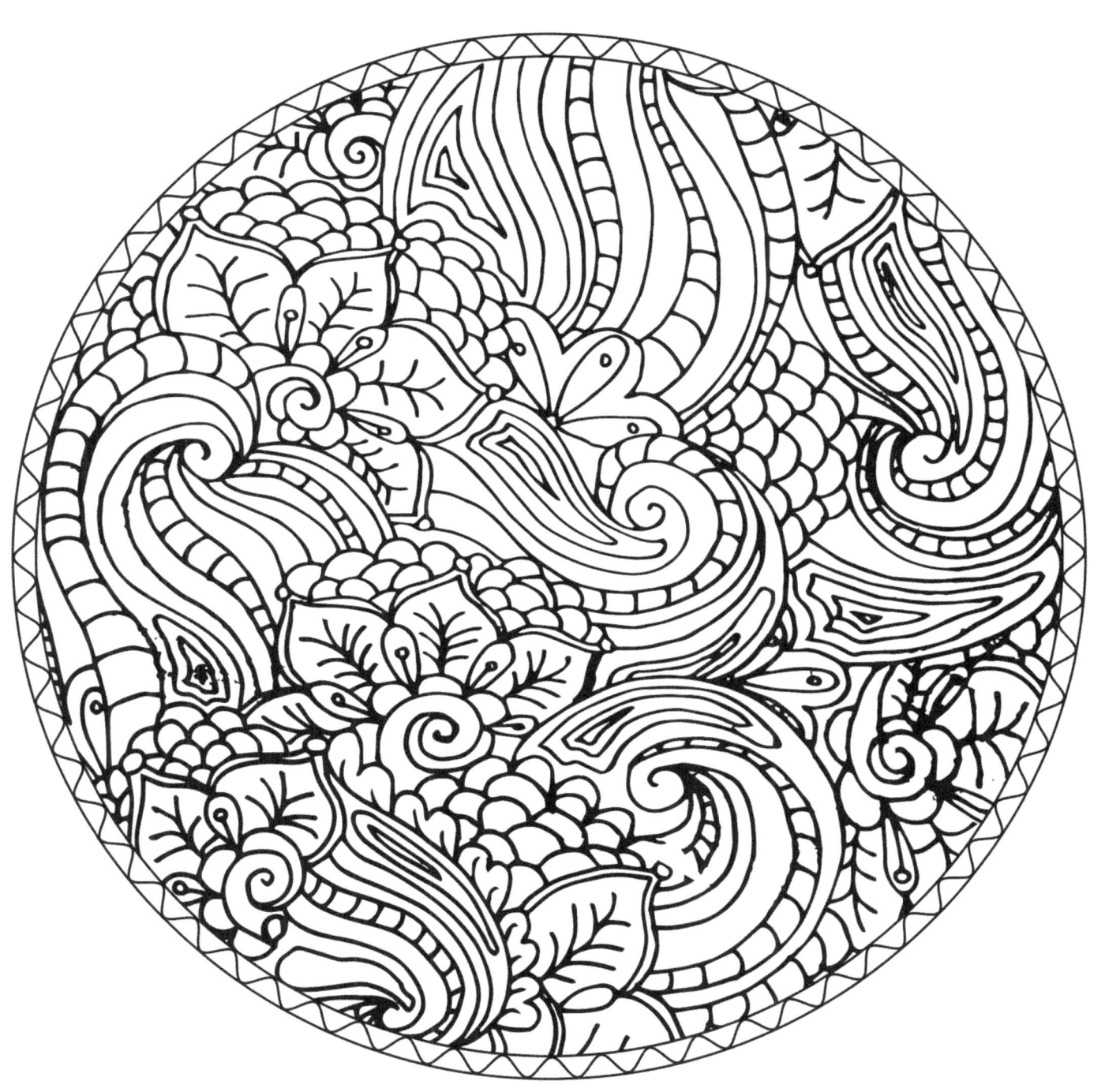

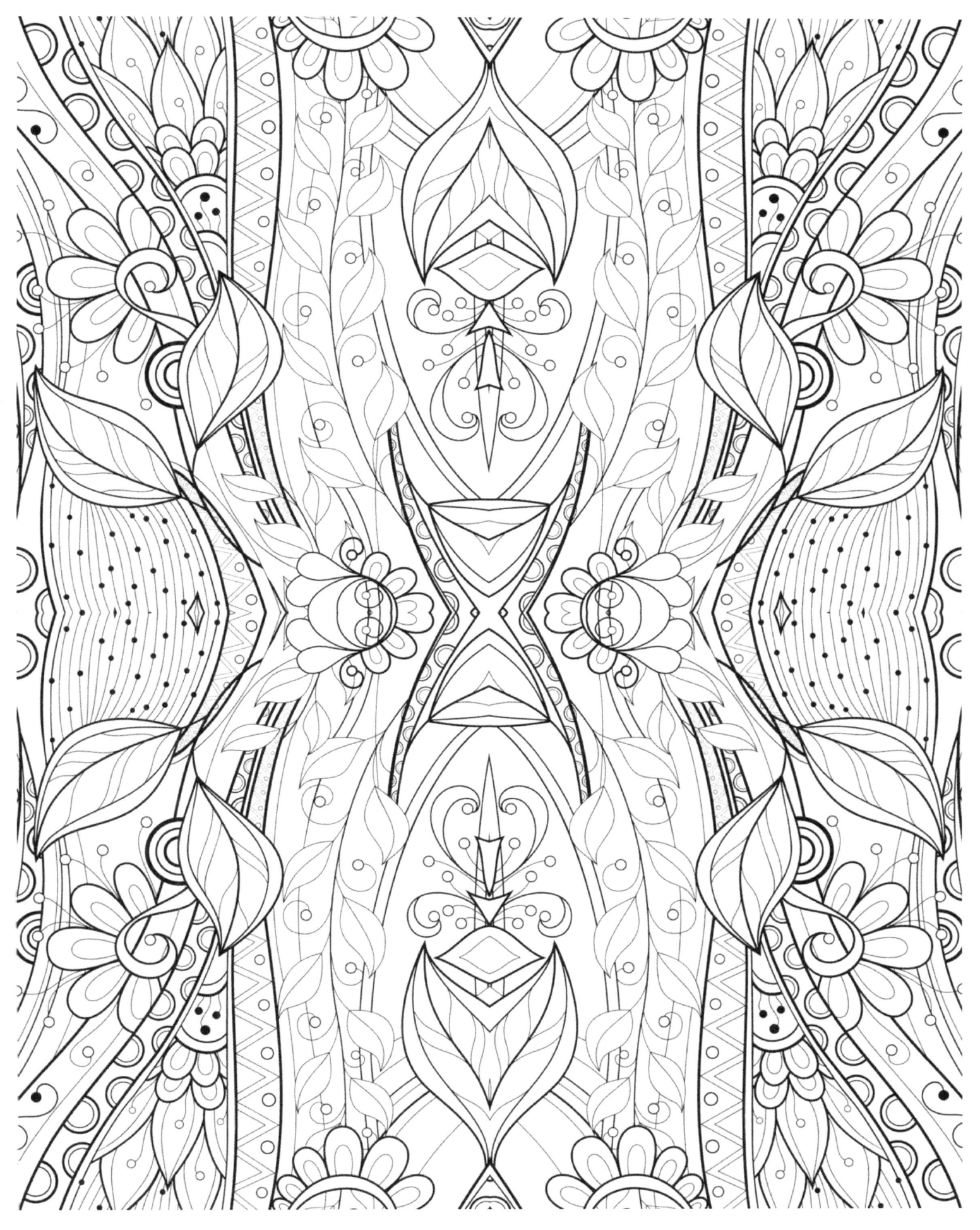

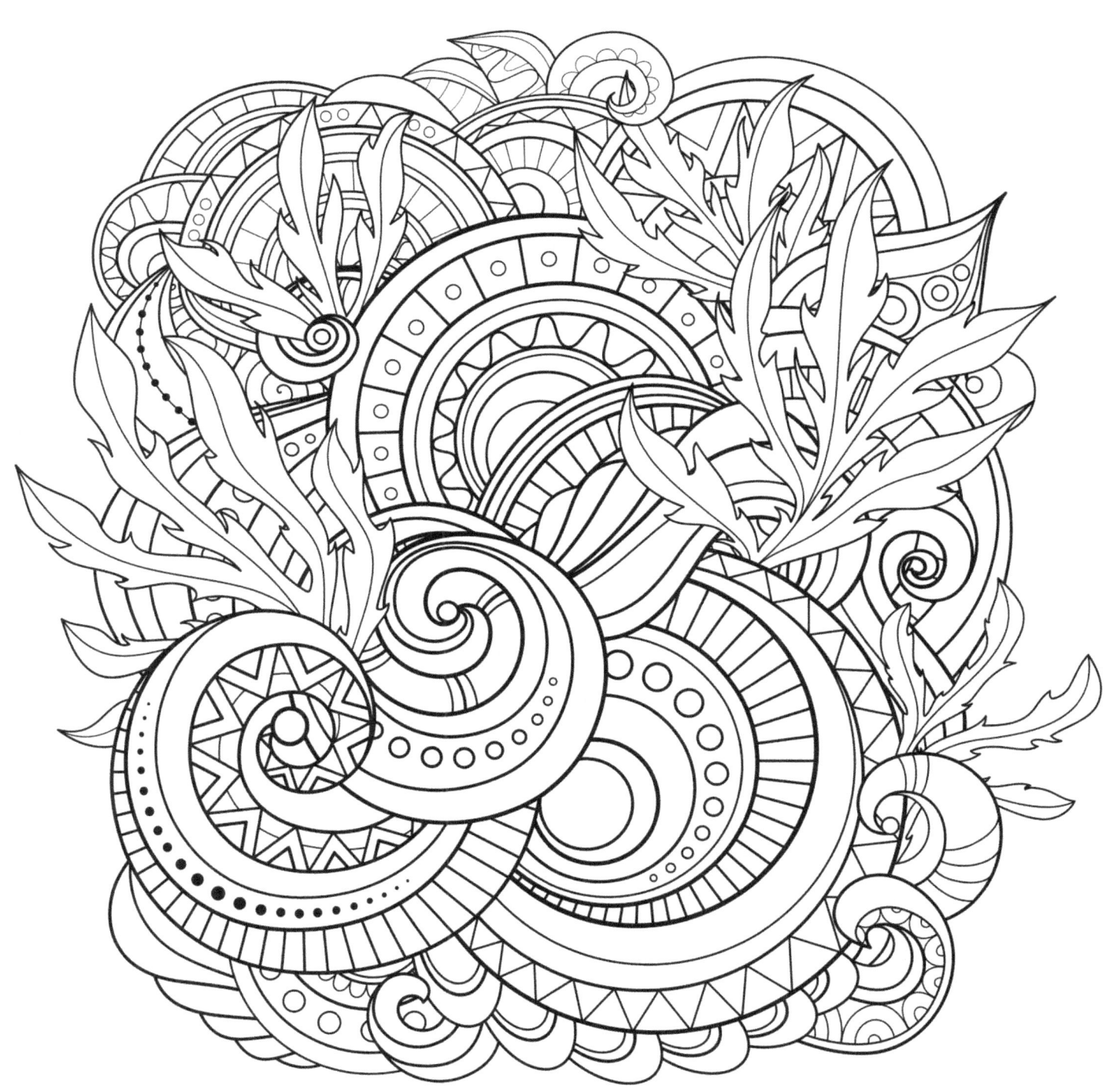

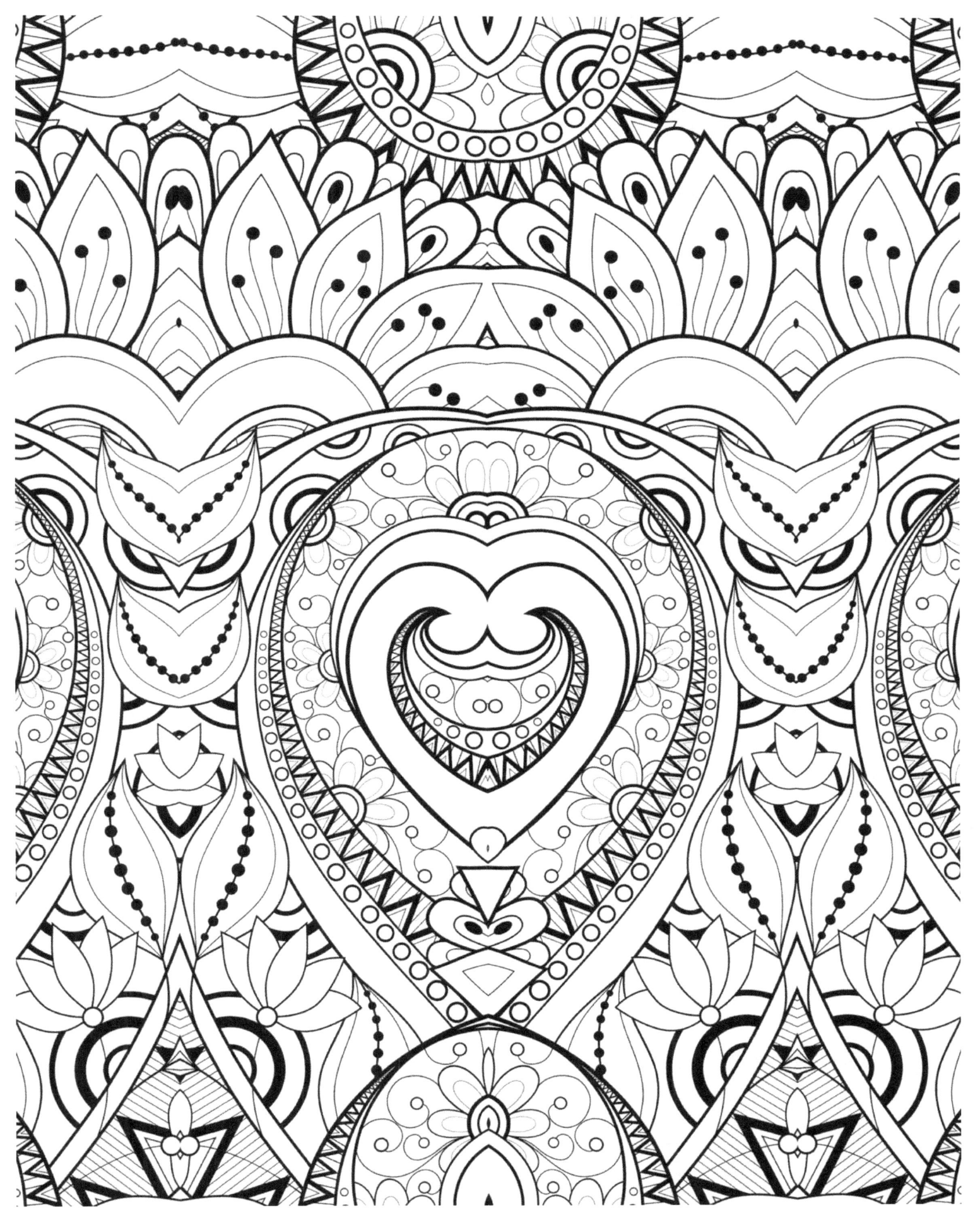

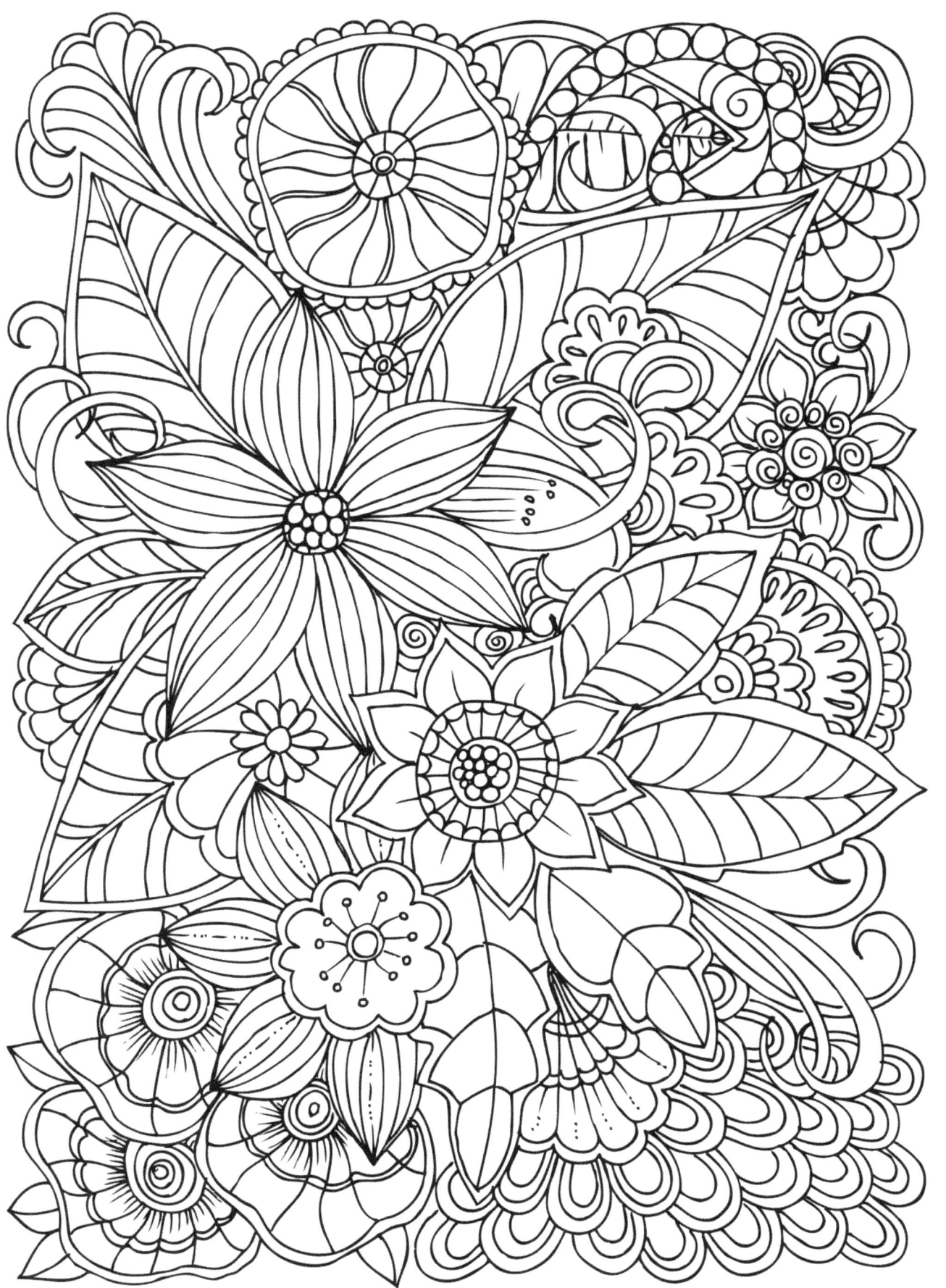

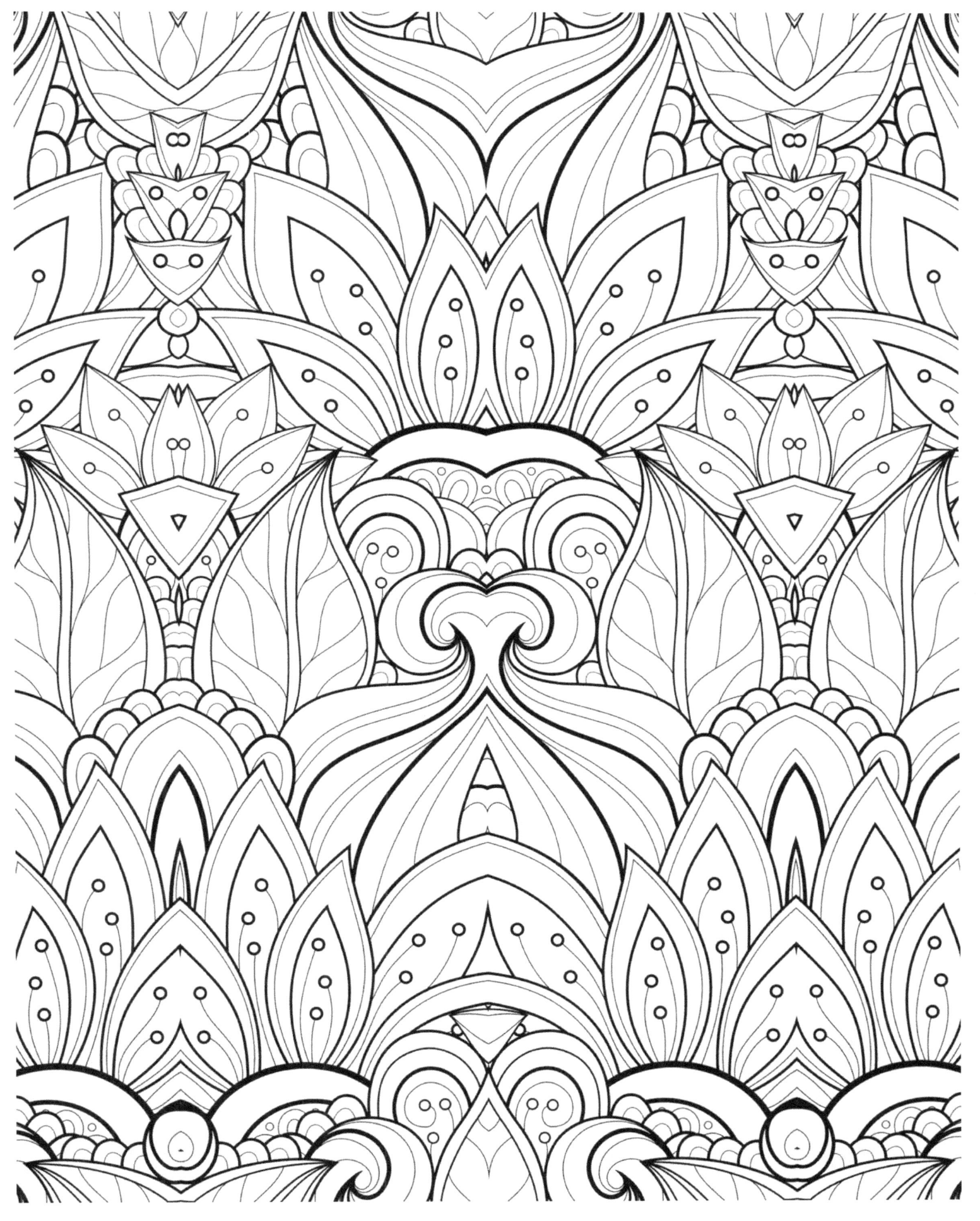

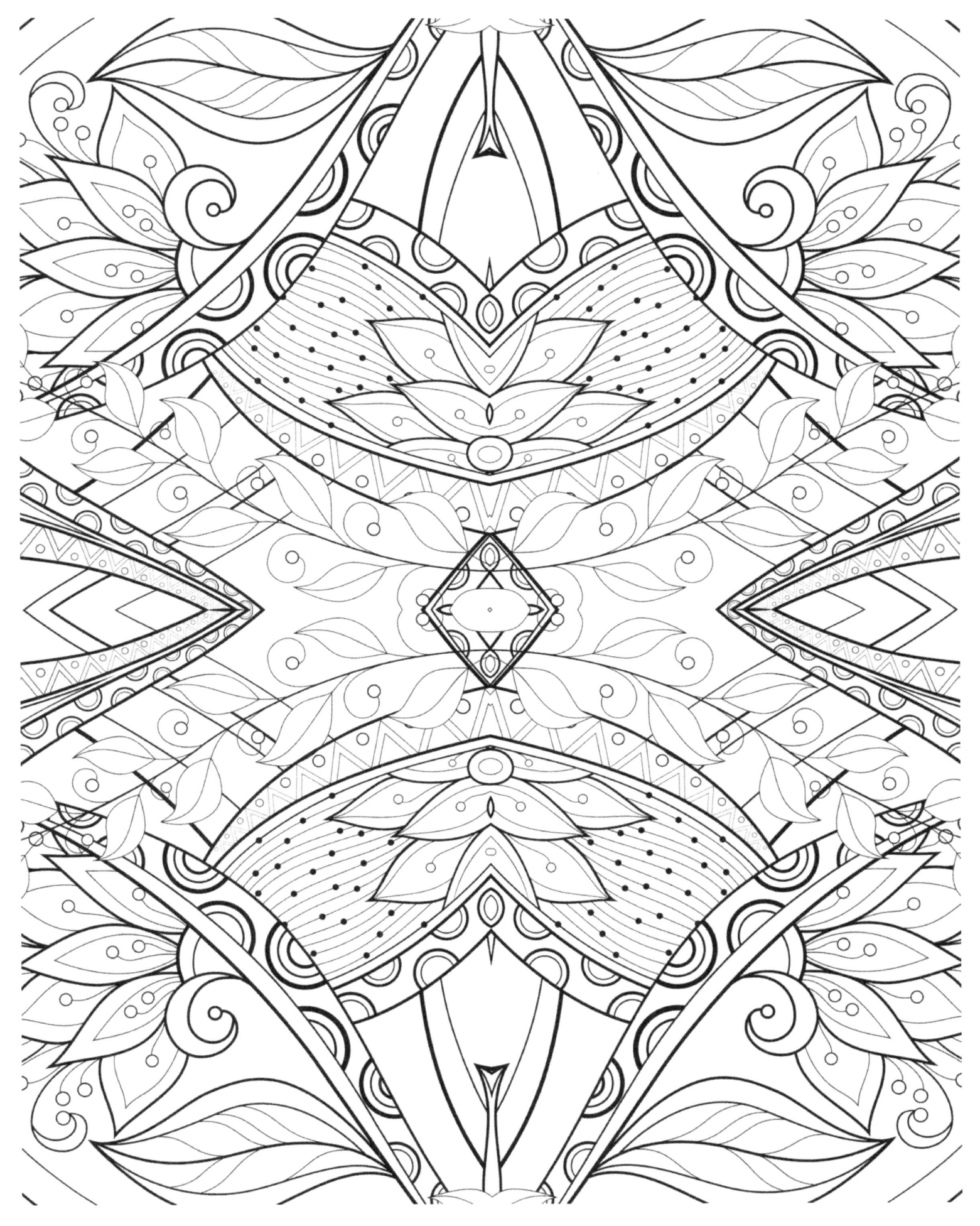

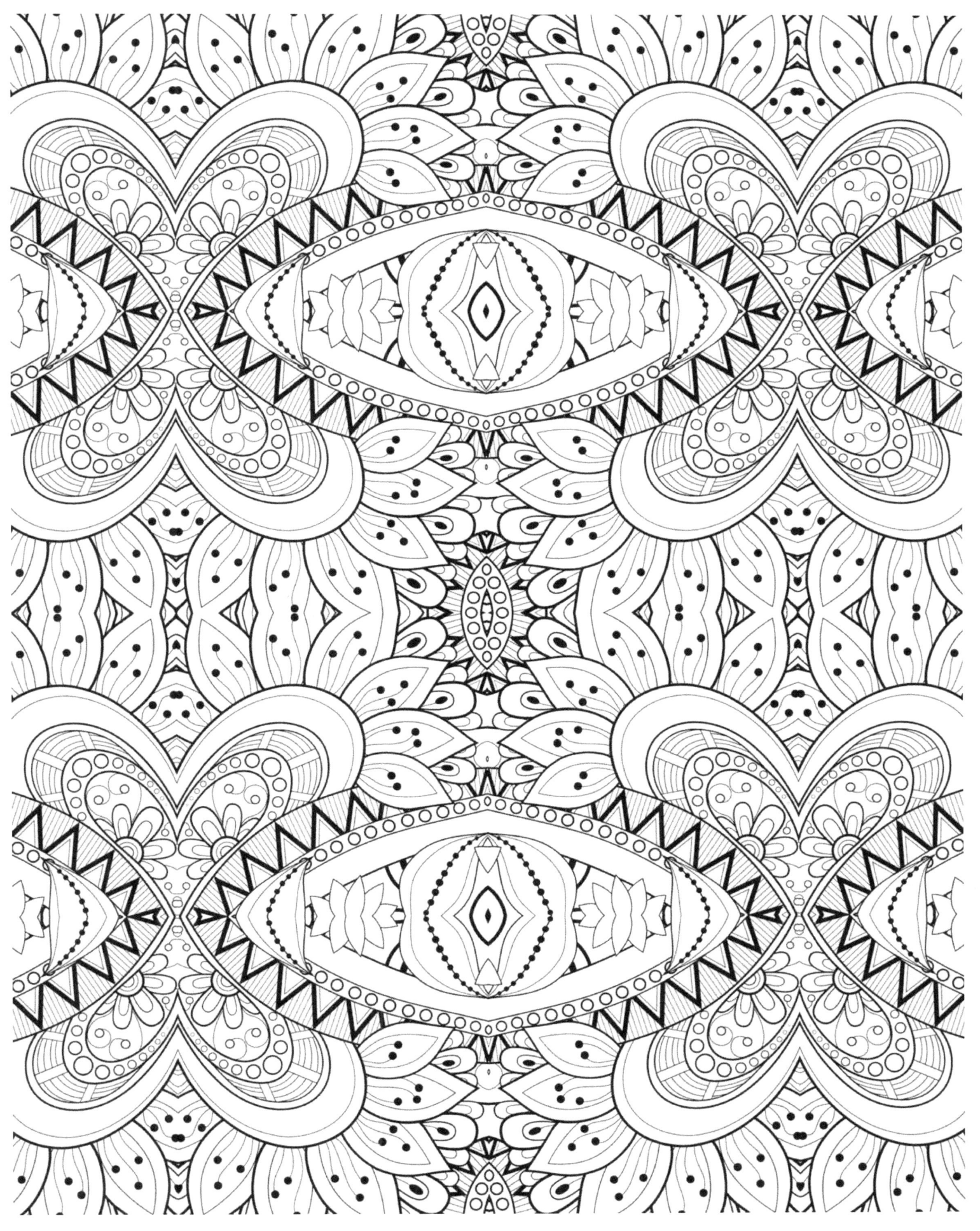

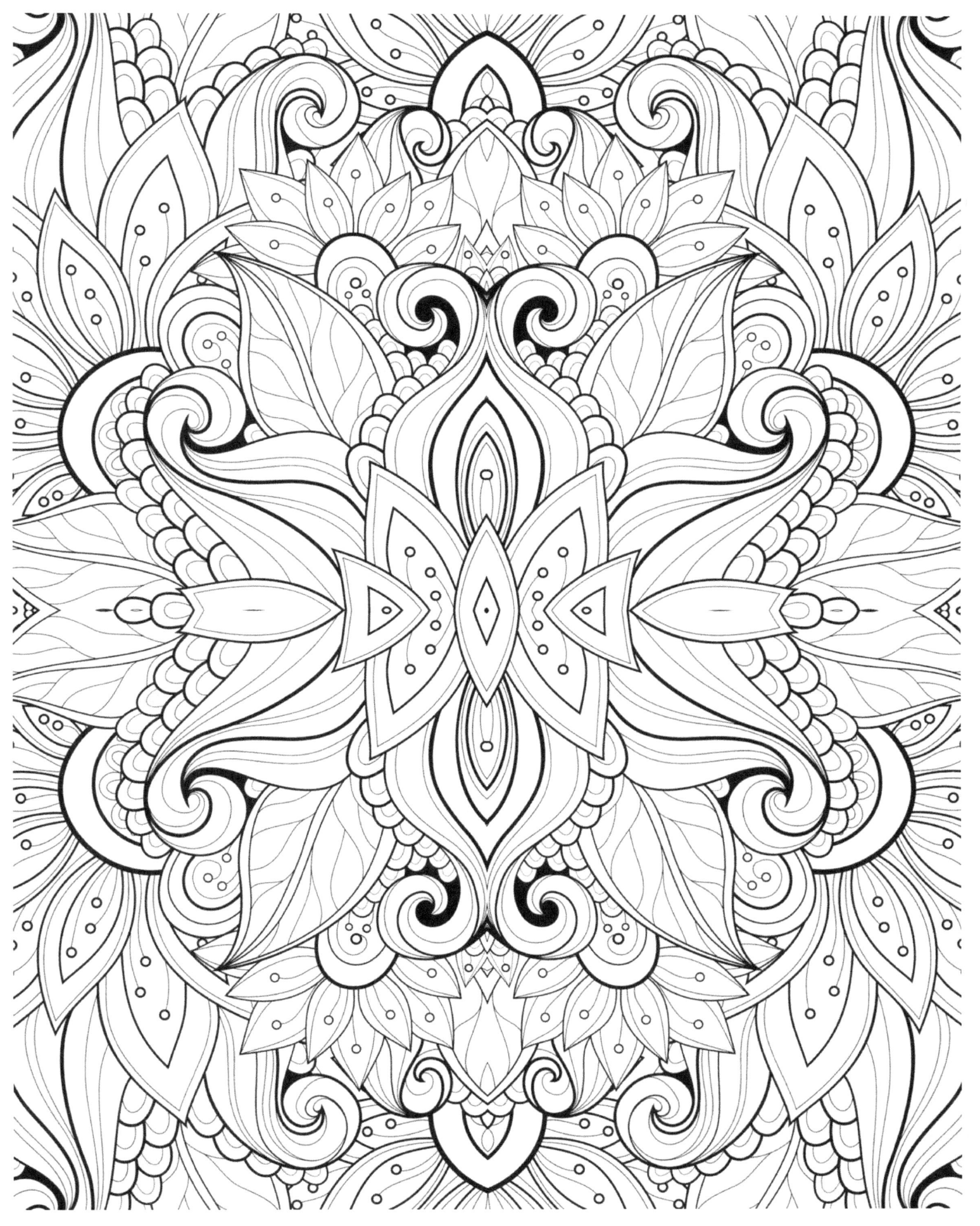

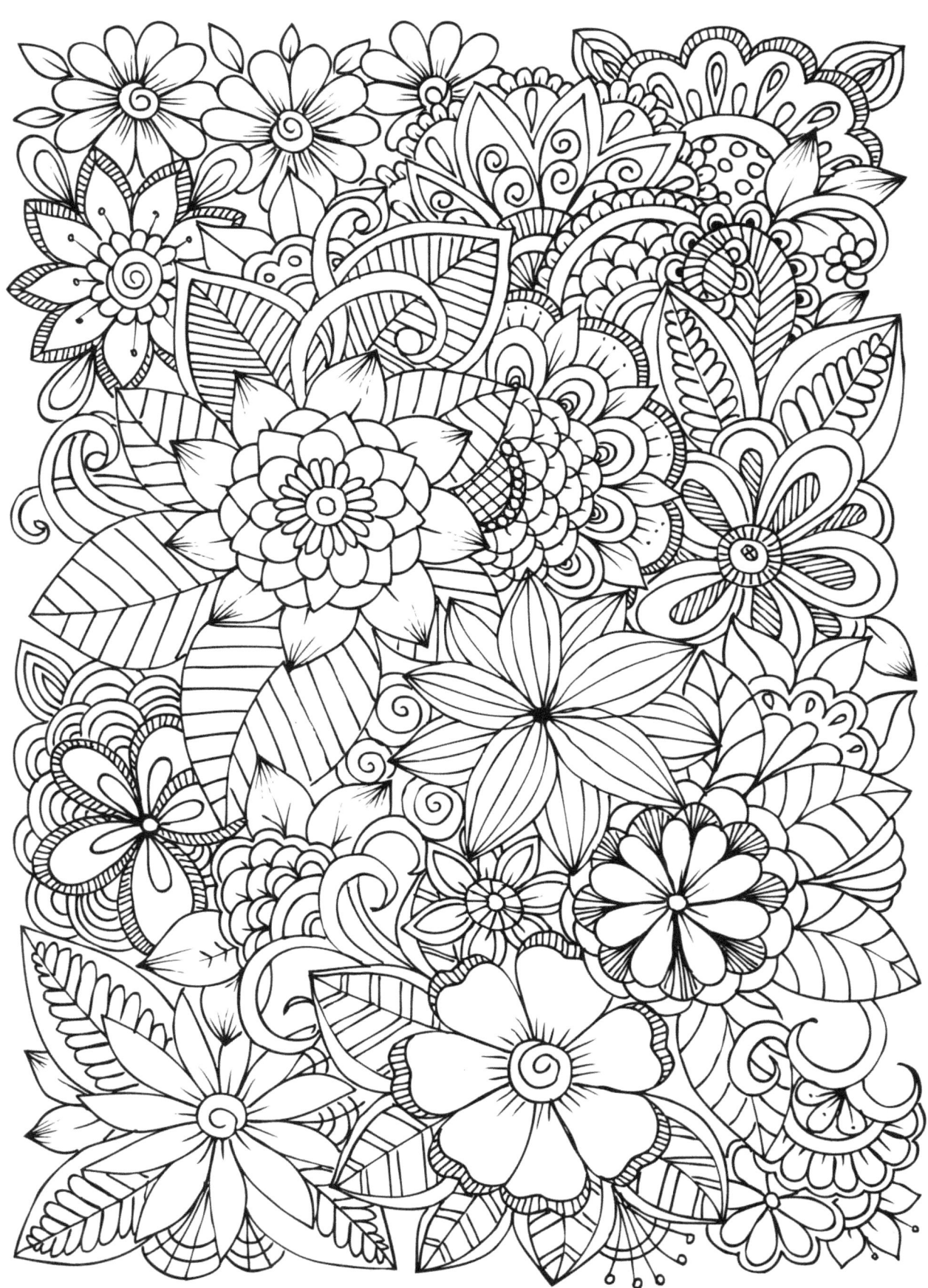

www.ingramcontent.com/pod-product-compliance
Lightning Source LLC
Chambersburg PA
CBHW081155280526
45787CB00008B/3337